Rookie reader®

Hello, Doctor

By
David F. Marx

Illustrated by
Mark A. Hicks

Children's Press®
A Division of Grolier Publishing
New York • London • Hong Kong • Sydney
Danbury, Connecticut

For Mark E.
—M. A. H.

Reading Consultants
Linda Cornwell
Coordinator of School Quality and Professional Improvement
(Indiana State Teachers Association)

Katharine A. Kane
Education Consultant
(Retired, San Diego County Office of Education
and San Diego State University)

Library of Congress Cataloging-in-Publication Data
Marx, David F.
    Hello, doctor / by David F. Marx ; illustrated by Mark A. Hicks.
        p. cm.—(Rookie reader)
    Summary: A little boy does everything the doctor tells him to do when he goes
for his check-up.
    ISBN 0-516-22033-0 (lib. bdg.)   0-516-27076-1 (pbk.)
    [1. Medical care—Fiction.] I. Hicks, Mark A., ill. II. Title. III. Series.
PZ7.M36822 He 2000
[E]—dc21   99-057171

Hello, doctor.

Tell me what to do.

I can "Ahhh!"

I can look.

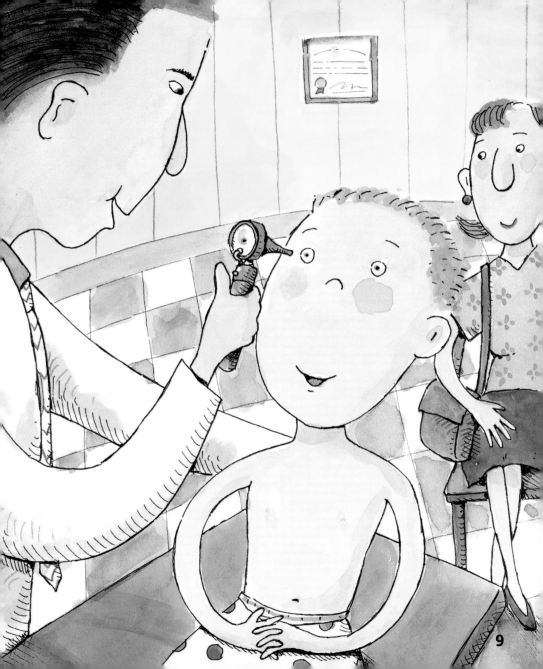

I can blow.

11

I can kick.

I can bend.

15

I can "go."

17

But can I do this?
What if it hurts?

Good. It's over.
I was brave.

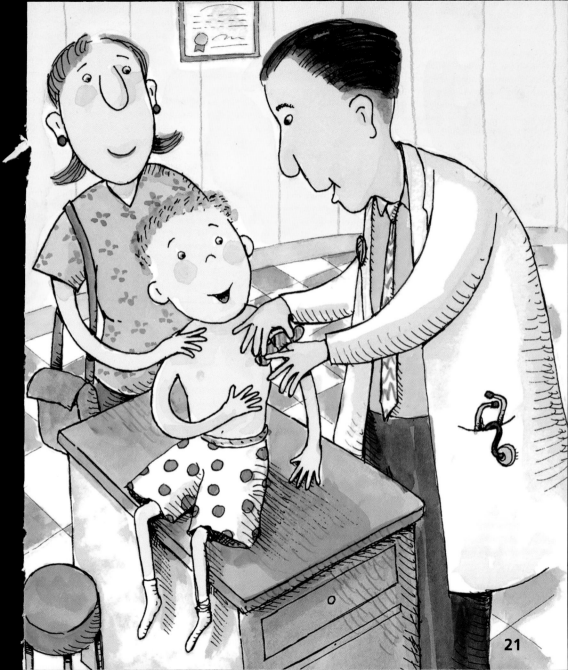

Thank you, doctor.
Goodbye.

Word List (28 words)

ahhh	good	look
bend	goodbye	me
blow	hello	over
brave	hurts	tell
but	I	thank
can	if	this
do	it	to
doctor	it's	was
go	kick	what
		you

About the Author

David F. Marx is a children's author and editor who lives in the Chicago area. He is the author of several other books in the Rookie Reader and Rookie Read-About Geography series for Children's Press.

About the Illustrator

Illustrator Mark A. Hicks has created award-winning artwork for books, magazines, and paper products.